10-16

SAD
ANIMAL
FACTS

Red squirrels
live alone.

SAD

ANIMAL

FACTS

BROOKE BARKER

FLATIRON
BOOKS
NEW YORK

www.flatironbooks.com

Designed by Steven Seighman
Production manager: Adriana Coada

The Library of Congress Cataloging-in-Publication Data is available upon request.

ISBN 978-1-250-09508-4 (hardcover)
ISBN 978-1-250-09509-1 (e-book)

Our books may be purchased in bulk for promotional, educational, or business use. Please contact your local bookseller or the Macmillan Corporate and Premium Sales Department at (800) 221-7945, extension 5442, or by e-mail at MacmillanSpecialMarkets@macmillan.com.

First Edition: September 2016

10   9   8   7   6   5   4   3   2   1

*For Boaz, if you were a grasshopper
you could jump over a two-story building.*

INTRODUCTION

"May you be a friend to every creature" was my grand-mother's creepy inscription in the Animal Babies book she gave me the day I was born.

I wanted her words to be prophetic, but my parents wouldn't let me have any pets and the nearest wilderness was annoyingly far away from our apartment complex in a Toronto suburb. So I settled for a childhood spent reading everything I could about animals.

What I learned wasn't always pretty. Just because our four-legged friends are soft and cute and often have amazing abilities doesn't mean they aren't also incredibly sad. Everyone knows that pigs are pink and have curly tails, but did you know that they can't see the sky? Sea turtles are majestic, but did you know that they never meet their parents, or that octopi don't have friends, jellyfish have no hearts, and zebras can't fall asleep alone? Animals, it turns out, are just as complicated and conflicted as we are.

I couldn't stop reading about those sad little animals. I was obsessed. In third grade I had to leave a birthday party after a horrible run-in with a hive of honeybees. "Every one of these stings is a bee that died," I informed my friend's mom as she drove me home from the last party I got invited to that year.

A few summers ago, at the end of an uneventful seven-hour whale-watching cruise (we saw zero whales), our captain apologized to us for the hundredth time while we stared at a part of the ocean that looked like all the other parts of the ocean. I thought about how, if a whale sings at the wrong frequency, he can't find any other whales because they can't hear his off-key song. His whole life is a failed whale-watching trip.

The more I learned about animals, the harder it was for me to keep quiet about them. A few years ago I was a reference librarian. It's not as thrilling as it sounds. It was a pretty slow job in a quiet place, and I passed a lot of the time by drawing animals on the backs of old card catalog slips. Each of my coworkers would suggest an animal at the end of their shift, and I'd draw it on the back of a catalog slip and leave it in the break room at the end of the day. I'd try to go out of my way to add to the drawing some new piece of knowledge about the animal (king cobras can spit venom nine feet), and they'd try to go out of their way to request animals I'd never heard of (monkfish, indri lemurs).

The more I read, the harder it is not to see these animals talking and complaining about their lives the way we do. The giraffe baby that falls six feet the moment it's born must think, "This is already off to a bad start," and worms with nine hearts must wish they only had someone to love.

There is a sad fact for every animal on earth, from fish and reptiles to cetaceans (marine mammals) and pinnipeds (a fancy word for seals and their cousins). There are animals that eat their own tails, that can't recognize their face in a mirror, and that force themselves to cry.

I hope this book doesn't force you to cry, and I hope it brings you closer to an animal in your life. Animals can use all the friends they can get. Sometimes they use them for food.

REPTILES AND AMPHIBIANS

AN ALLIGATOR'S BRAIN
WEIGHS LESS THAN
AN OREO.

LONG-TAILED SKINKS EAT THEIR OWN EGGS.

FROGS CAN CLOSE THEIR EARS.

TURTLES BREATHE OUT THEIR BUTTS.

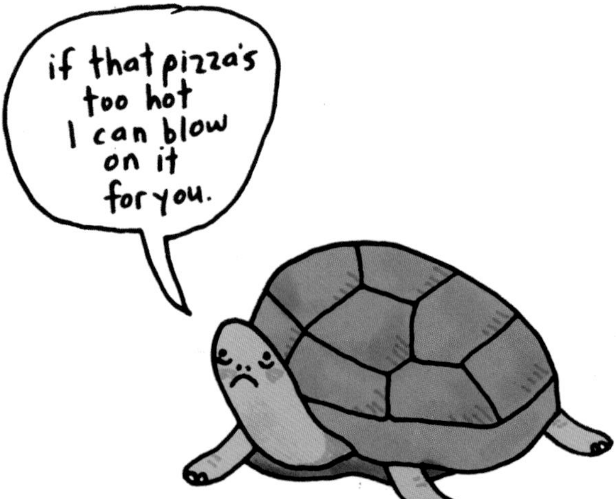
if that pizza's too hot I can blow on it for you.

PIT VIPERS HAVE HEAT SENSORS
ON THEIR MOUTHS.

MARINE IGUANAS SNEEZE OUT SALT
WHEN THEY EAT TOO MUCH OF IT.

FIRE SALAMANDERS EAT THEIR SIBLINGS

CROCODILES LIVED WITH DINOSAURS.

WATER-HOLDING FROGS EAT THEIR
OWN SKIN FOR NUTRIENTS.

WHEN STAR TORTOISE EGGS
HATCH AT COLD TEMPERATURES
MORE MALES ARE BORN,
AND AT WARM TEMPERATURES
MORE FEMALES ARE BORN.

GARDEN LIZARDS EAT
THEIR OWN TAILS
FOR CALCIUM.

SEA TURTLES NEVER
MEET THEIR MOMS.

STRAWBERRY POISON DART FROGS
FEED THEIR UNFERTILIZED EGGS
TO THEIR HATCHED BABIES.

MAMMALS

LITTLE BROWN BATS
ARE AWAKE FOR
4 HOURS A DAY.

THE RING-TAILED LEMUR
THAT SMELLS THE WORST
IS IN CHARGE OF THE
ENTIRE GROUP.

CAMELS CAN DRINK 30 GALLONS OF WATER IN 15 MINUTES.

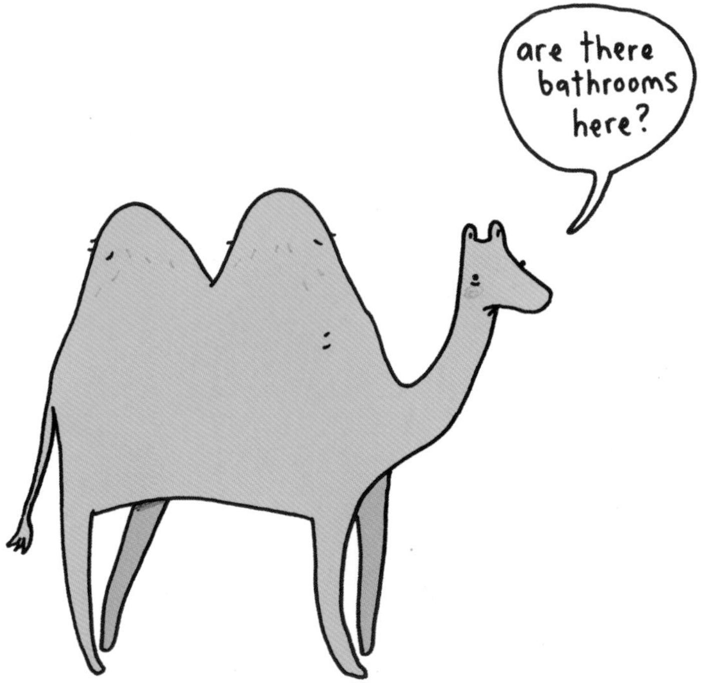
are there bathrooms here?

HYENAS EAT ROTTING MEAT.

SEA OTTERS LIVE IN
ALMOST-FREEZING WATER
THAT WOULD KILL A
HUMAN IN AN HOUR.

BATS HAVE LONG-DISTANCE
RELATIONSHIPS.

COLOBUS MONKEY STOMACHS CAN HANDLE
FOOD THAT NO ONE ELSE WILL EAT.

SHEEP CAN ONLY REMEMBER 50 FACES.

RHINOS MAKE A SQUEAKING SOUND
TO CALL FOR THEIR FRIENDS

FOXES LIVE, WORK, EAT, AND SLEEP ALONE.

HIPPOS ATTRACT MATES BY PEEING.

BOY PUPPIES LET GIRL PUPPIES
WIN WHEN THEY PLAYFIGHT.

PIGS HAVE TROUBLE
SEEING THE SKY BECAUSE
OF HOW THEIR EYES
ARE PLACED.

TARSIER EYES ARE BIGGER
THAN THEIR STOMACHS.

WILD YAKS EAT SNOW
TO STAY HYDRATED

ZEBRAS CAN'T
SLEEP ALONE.

IF A WOLF IS KICKED
OUT OF ITS PACK

IT NEVER HOWLS AGAIN.

RACCOON HANDS ARE NIMBLE
ENOUGH TO STEAL A DIME
FROM YOUR POCKET

PRAIRIE DOGS HAVE DIFFERENT CALLS
TO COMMUNICATE DIFFERENT
HUMAN HEIGHTS AND HUMAN
SHIRT COLORS, BUT CAN'T
DIFFERENTIATE BETWEEN
CIRCLES AND SQUARES.

IF A FEMALE FERRET GOES
INTO HEAT AND DOESN'T MATE
SHE WILL DIE.

A CHIPMUNK CAN'T RECOGNIZE
ITS FACE IN A MIRROR.

SLOTHS COME DOWN FROM THEIR TREES
ONCE A WEEK TO USE THE BATHROOM.

GOATS CAN SEE
ALMOST 360° AROUND THEM.

ARMADILLOS CAN'T KEEP
THEMSELVES WARM
AND FORM GROUPS
WHEN THE
TEMPERATURE DROPS.

A FEMALE FISHER CAN BE
PREGNANT FOR
350 DAYS IN A YEAR.

ELEPHANT BABIES SUCK ON THEIR TRUNKS
THE WAY HUMAN BABIES SUCK ON THEIR THUMBS.

A FEMALE BLACK BEAR CAN HIBERNATE
UP TO EIGHT MONTHS.

GROUNDHOG DAY WAS
HEDGEHOG DAY UNTIL
THE 1800's.

PREGNANT POLAR BEARS GAIN 500 POUNDS

GUACAMOLE IS EXTREMELY
POISONOUS TO HAMSTERS.

MALE LIONS EAT FIRST
AND MAKE THE WOMEN
AND CHILDREN EAT LAST.

PANDAS DON'T HAVE
SET SLEEPING AREAS
THEY JUST FALL ASLEEP
WHEREVER THEY ARE.

COWS PRODUCE THE MOST MILK
WHEN THEY LISTEN TO
R.E.M.'s "EVERYBODY HURTS."

MOOSE EAT FOR 8 HOURS A DAY.

my main hobbies are trees and shrubs.

MICE CAN SENSE SADNESS
IN OTHER MICE AND IT
MAKES THEM SAD TOO.

HYRAXES HAVE 30 DIFFERENT CALLS.

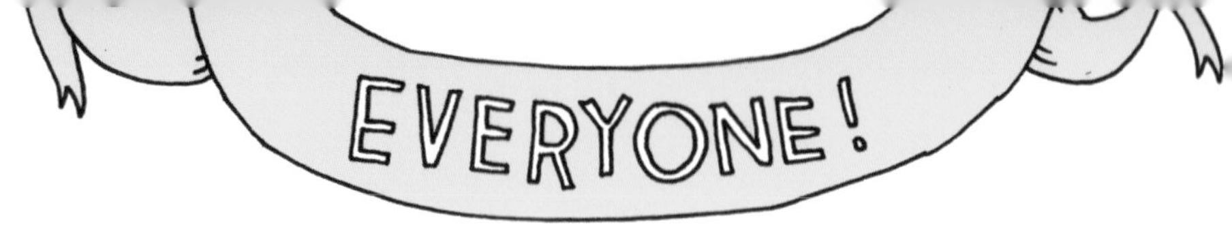
EVERYONE!

ALL GNU ARE BORN
DURING A 3-WEEK PERIOD.

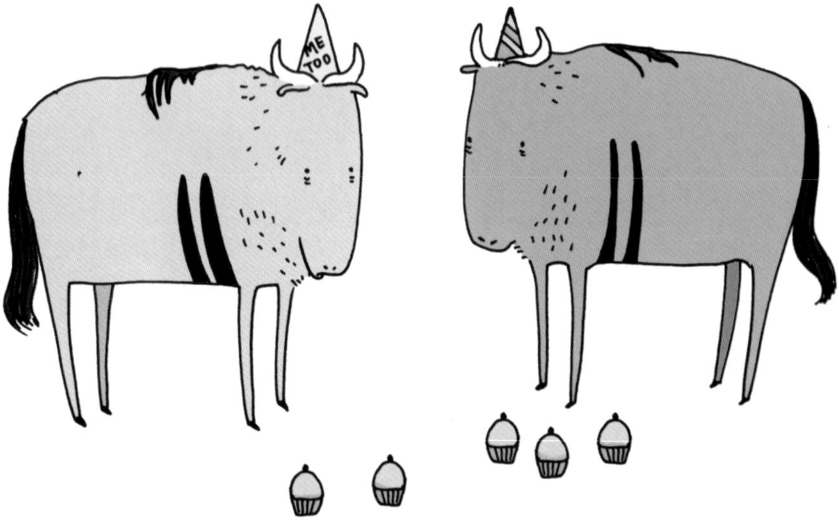
ME TOO

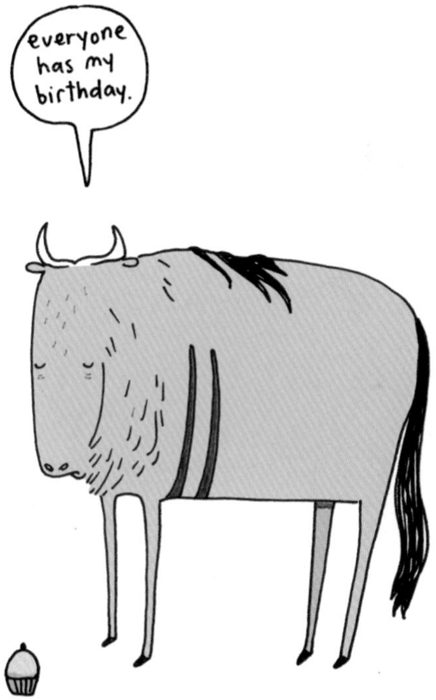
everyone has my birthday.

SNOW LEOPARDS EAT
20 POUNDS OF FOOD A NIGHT.

PUMAS, MOUNTAIN LIONS,
AND COUGARS
ARE ALL THE SAME ANIMAL.

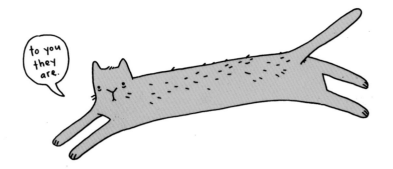

GUINEA PIGS SLEEP
WITH THEIR EYES OPEN.

DOMESTICATED RABBITS
LIVE 8 YEARS AS PETS
OR 24 HOURS ON THEIR OWN.

TWO DOGS WERE HANGED
FOR WITCHCRAFT DURING
THE SALEM WITCH TRIALS.

POLYDACTYL CATS HAVE THUMBS
BUT THEY AREN'T OPPOSABLE

DIKDIKS MARK
THEIR TERRITORY
WITH THEIR TEARS.

GIBBON CALLS CAN BE HEARD 2 MILES AWAY.

FENNEC FOX EARS TAKE UP A THIRD OF THEIR BODY.

COUGARS CAN'T ROAR BUT THEY CAN SCREAM.

15 MARA FAMILIES LIVE IN ONE BURROW.

GIRAFFES SLEEP
3 HOURS A NIGHT.

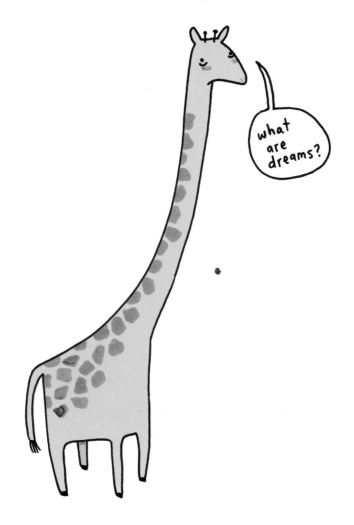

ANTEATERS CAN BE AS BIG AS HUMANS,
BUT THE INSIDE OF THEIR MOUTH
IS THE SIZE OF AN OLIVE.

DOGS CAN'T SEE TELEVISION BUT THEY
PRETEND TO LIKE IT SO THEY
CAN BE CLOSE TO YOU.

APES TELL LIES.

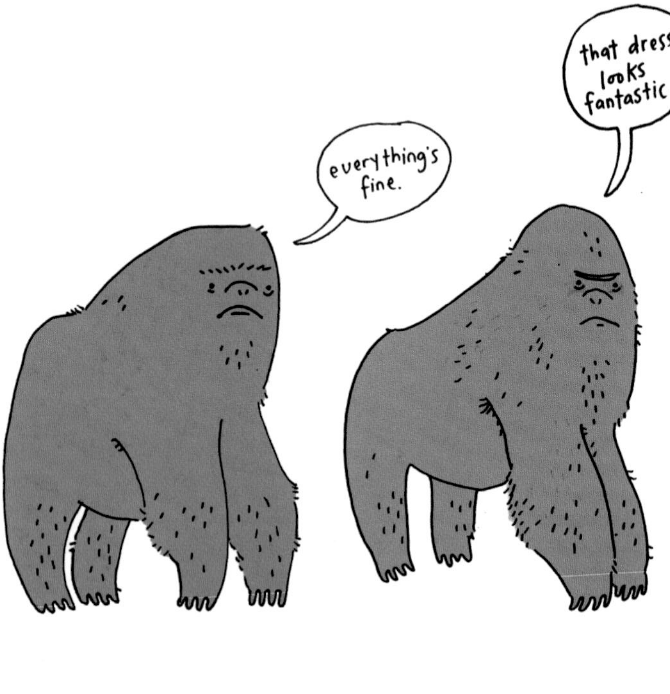
everything's fine.
that dress looks fantastic.

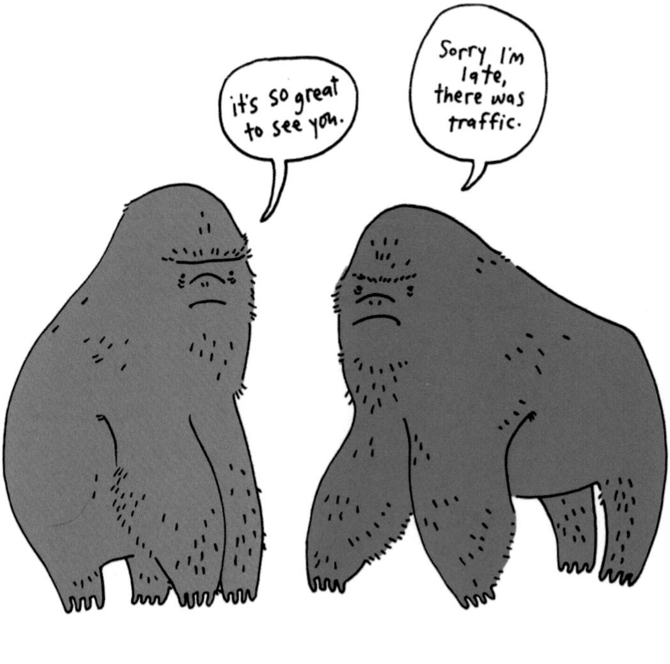
it's so great to see you.
Sorry I'm late, there was traffic.

DWARF LEMURS LINE THEIR HOMES WITH FECES.

CITY COYOTES LIVE LONGER THAN
COYOTES IN THE WILDERNESS.

TIGERS DON'T LIKE
MAKING EYE CONTACT
WHILE THEY HUNT.

RED RUFFED LEMURS LEAVE
THEIR KIDS WHEN THEY
GO LOOK FOR FOOD.

I love
you but
I need
a snack.

GORILLAS CAN CATCH HUMAN COLDS.

LAB RATS ENJOY MATING
MORE WHEN THEY'RE
WEARING VESTS.

MEERKAT BABIES ARE GIVEN
DEAD SCORPIONS TO PLAY WITH.

IF A CHINCHILLA GETS WET, IT MIGHT NEVER GET DRY

BEAVERS NEED TO CHEW CONSTANTLY
BECAUSE THEIR TEETH
NEVER STOP GROWING.

ELEPHANTS CAN'T JUMP.

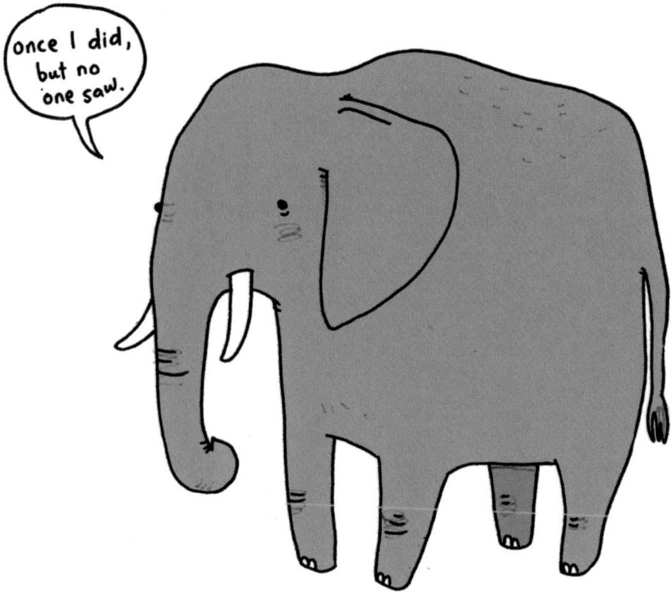
once I did, but no one saw.

HORSES THAT LOOK LIKE THEY'RE SMILING
ARE ACTUALLY SMELLING THE AIR.

NEWBORN PORCUPINES ARE READY
TO INJURE SOMEONE WITHIN
MINUTES OF BEING BORN.

SQUIRRELS CAN'T BURP.

for the last time, that wasn't me.

GIRAFFE BABIES FALL
6 FEET TO THE GROUND
WHEN THEY'RE BORN.

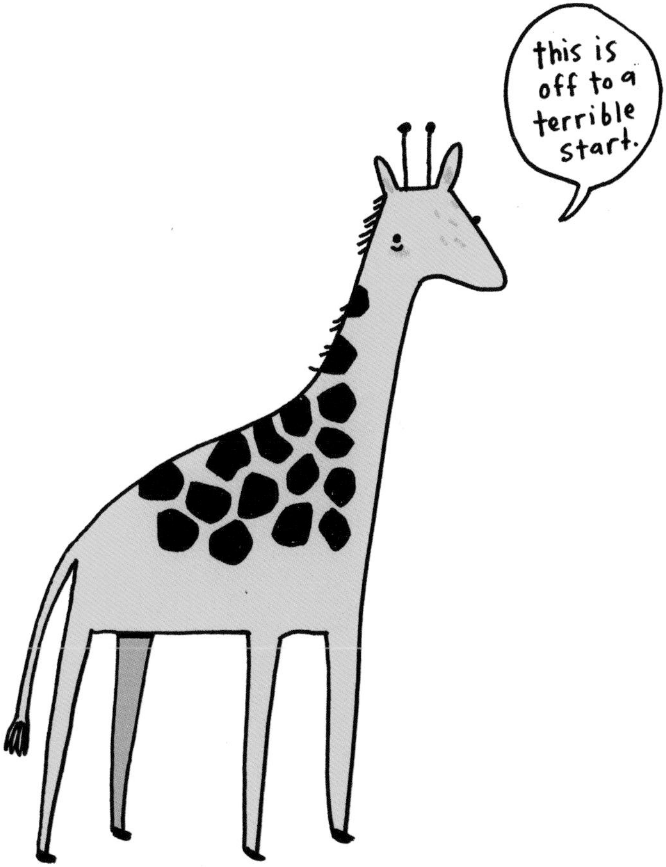
this is off to a terrible start.

A PLATYPUS SWIMS WITH ITS EYES CLOSED.

MARSUPIALS
(they're mammals too)

KANGAROOS COUGH TO SHOW SUBMISSION.

OPOSSUM MOMS CARRY
THEIR CHILDREN
ON THEIR BACKS.

KOALAS ARE ONLY SOCIAL
FOR 15 MINUTES A DAY.

AFTER TASMANIAN DEVILS MATE,
THE FEMALE SNEAKS AWAY IN THE NIGHT.

marine mammals:

CETACEANS
AND
PINNIPEDS

BABY WHALES GAIN
200 POUNDS A DAY.

WALRUSES BREATHE ON THE OCEAN FLOOR TO UNCOVER FOOD HIDDEN IN THE SAND.

WHEN EARLY OCEAN EXPLORERS
THOUGHT THEY SAW MERMAIDS
THEY WERE ACTUALLY LOOKING
AT MANATEES.

WHALES THAT SING
IN THE WRONG KEY
GET LOST AND ARE
ALONE IN THE OCEAN.

NARWHAL MEANS "CORPSE WHALE"
BECAUSE OF THEIR BLOTCHY,
TRANSLUCENT SKIN.

MONK SEALS CAN'T DREAM UNDERWATER.

ONLY HALF A DOLPHIN'S BRAIN SLEEPS AT A TIME.

HARP SEAL PUPS
ARE ABANDONED
ON BEACHES AT BIRTH,
AND 30% DON'T SURVIVE.

FISH

CLOWNFISH HAVE A SLIMY MUCUS COATING.

SHARK PREGNANCIES CAN LAST YEARS.

KOI FISH CAN LIVE 200 YEARS.

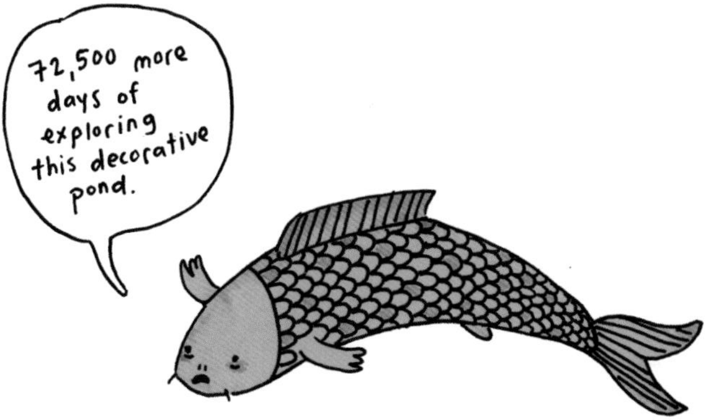
72,500 more days of exploring this decorative pond.

GUPPIES CAN'T TAKE NAPS.
BECAUSE THEY DON'T
HAVE EYELIDS.

SEAHORSES ARE ONE OF THE
ONLY ANIMALS WHERE THE
MALES BECOME PREGNANT.

NURSE SHARKS LOSE A TOOTH A WEEK.

HERRINGS COMMUNICATE WITH FARTS.

MOSQUITOFISH CAN ONLY
COUNT TO 100.

BLOBFISH HAVE NO MUSCLES.

HAMMERHEAD SHARKS
CAN SMELL ELECTRICITY.

BIRDS

BIRDS CAN'T GO TO SPACE
BECAUSE THEY NEED
GRAVITY TO SWALLOW.

SCIENTISTS DON'T UNDERSTAND WHY
FLAMINGOS STAND ON ONE LEG.

BURROWING OWLS LAUGH WHEN THEY'RE AFRAID.

BALD EAGLES SAVE EVERYTHING THEY FIND
UNTIL THEIR NESTS FALL TO THE GROUND
BECAUSE THE TREES CAN'T SUPPORT THEIR WEIGHT.

IF HUMANS HAD THE METABOLISM
OF HUMMINGBIRDS, THEY'D HAVE
TO EAT 400 HAMBURGERS A DAY.

EMUS CAN'T WALK BACKWARD.

ADELIE PENGUINS PUSH
EACH OTHER OFF LEDGES
TO CHECK IF THE
WATER'S SAFE.

BARN OWLS ARE USUALLY MONOGAMOUS
BUT 25% OF COUPLES SEPARATE.

CROWS NEVER
FORGET
A FACE.

ANYTHING A DUCKLING MEETS WITHIN 10 MINUTES
OF BEING BORN BECOMES ITS PARENT.

BLACK EAGLES WATCH THEIR CHILDREN
FIGHT TO THE DEATH WITHOUT INTERFERING

PIGEONS PUT OFF THINGS
THEY DON'T WANT TO DO.

THE AVERAGE GOLDCREST LIVES 8 MONTHS.

IN CROWDED GROUPS OF
EMPEROR PENGUINS,
MATES FIND EACH OTHER
BY SMELL INSTEAD OF BY SIGHT.

KIWIS CAN REMEMBER A
BAD MEMORY FOR 5 YEARS.

HORNBILL CHICKS COME OUT OF THE NEST WHEN
THEY'RE A FEW DAYS OLD, THEN IMMEDIATELY
GO BACK IN FOR ANOTHER FEW MONTHS.

MALE PEACOCKS MAKE
FAKE MATING SOUNDS
TO ATTRACT FEMALES.

GREAT BRITAIN HAS INVESTED
HUNDREDS OF THOUSANDS OF
POUNDS TO FIND OUT WHY
SEAGULLS ATTACK SO MANY
PEOPLE AT OUTDOOR FESTIVALS.

OWLS CAN'T MOVE THEIR EYES
BECAUSE THEY DON'T HAVE
EYEBALLS, THEY HAVE EYE TUBES.

imagine I'm
rolling my
eyes at you.

HYACINTH MACAWS HAVE THE
INTELLIGENCE OF A 3-YEAR-OLD.

AN ALBATROSS CAN
PICK UP SMELLS
12 MILES AWAY.

WOODPECKER TONGUES WRAP
AROUND THE BACK OF THEIR BRAINS.

A SPARROW WILL EAT ANYTHING
THAT FITS IN ITS MOUTH.

ARACARI SLEEP WITH
THEIR HEADS
IN THEIR ARMPITS.

I have the
worst
morning
breath.

AN OSTRICH SPENDS
7 MONTHS ALONE
EVERY YEAR.

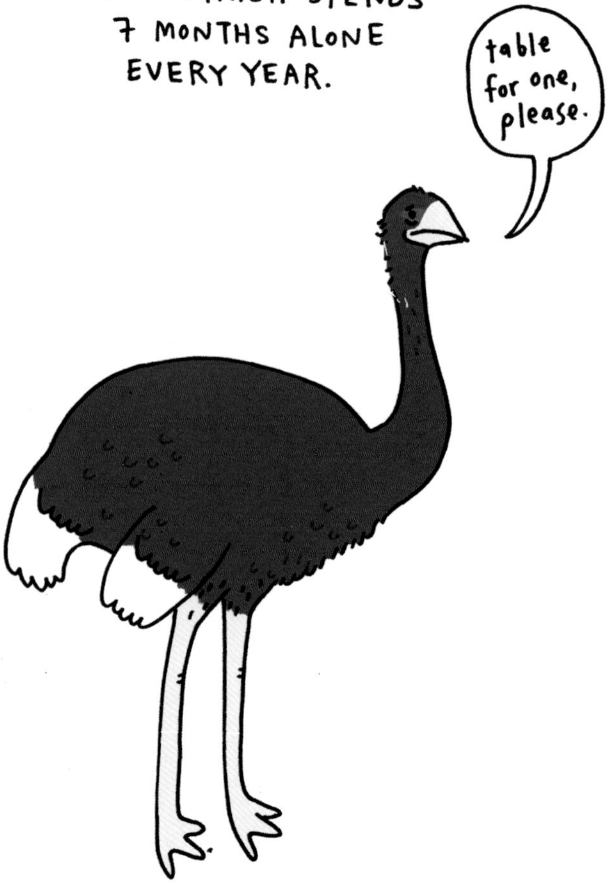
table for one, please.

MALE WHITE FRONT PARROTS
VOMIT ON FEMALES THEY
WANT TO MATE WITH.

ROADRUNNERS MAKE
THEMSELVES CRY TO
GET RID OF EXCESS SALT.

COOT PARENTS PECK
AT THEIR YOUNG IF
THEY ASK FOR FOOD.

INSECTS AND
ARACHNIDS

GIRL. CRICKETS CAN'T CHIRP.

MOTHS HAVE NO STOMACHS.

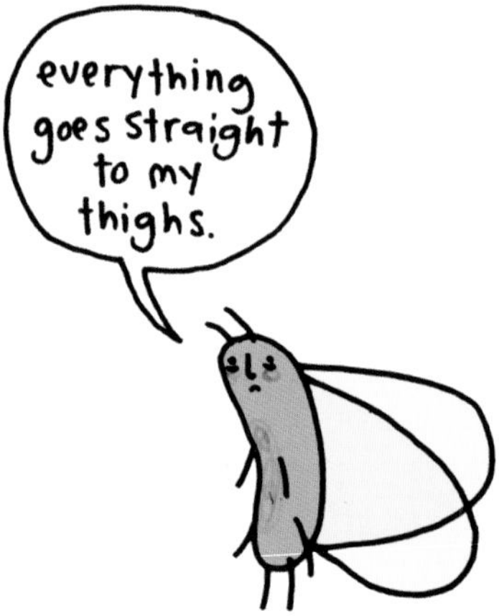
everything goes straight to my thighs.

THE AVERAGE MAYFLY
LIVES LESS THAN A DAY.

IF BEES EARNED MINIMUM WAGE
A JAR OF HONEY WOULD COST
$182,000.

ADULT FIREFLIES DON'T EAT.

SCORPIONS ARE NOCTURNAL HUNTERS
BUT THEY GLOW IN THE DARK.

ANTS DON'T SLEEP
BUT THEY TAKE
  8-MINUTE NAPS
  TWICE A DAY.

DRAGONFLY MIGRATION TAKES
FOUR GENERATIONS.

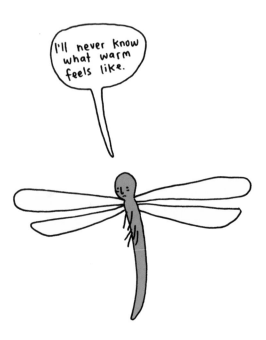

TARANTULAS CAN GO YEARS
WITHOUT EATING.

CICADAS STAY
UNDERGROUND
FOR 17 YEARS

HOUSEFLIES CAN ONLY HUM
IN THE KEY OF F.

SOME SPECIES OF SPIDERS
EAT THROUGH THEIR MOM
WHEN THEY'RE BORN.

BUTTERFLIES TASTE EVERYTHING
THEY WALK ON.

MISCELLANEOUS INVERTEBRATES

WORMS
HAVE
FIVE
HEARTS

and no one to love.

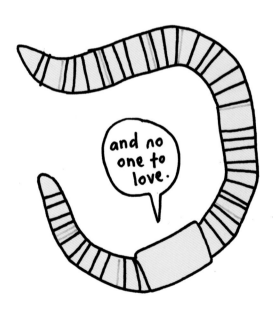

IF YOU CUT OFF A SNAIL'S EYE
IT WILL GROW BACK.

SECTIONS OF HIGHWAY ON
CHRISTMAS ISLAND ARE CLOSED
FOR RED CRAB MIGRATION.

AN OCTOPUS LIVES ALONE AND LEAVES HOME ONLY WHEN NECESSARY.

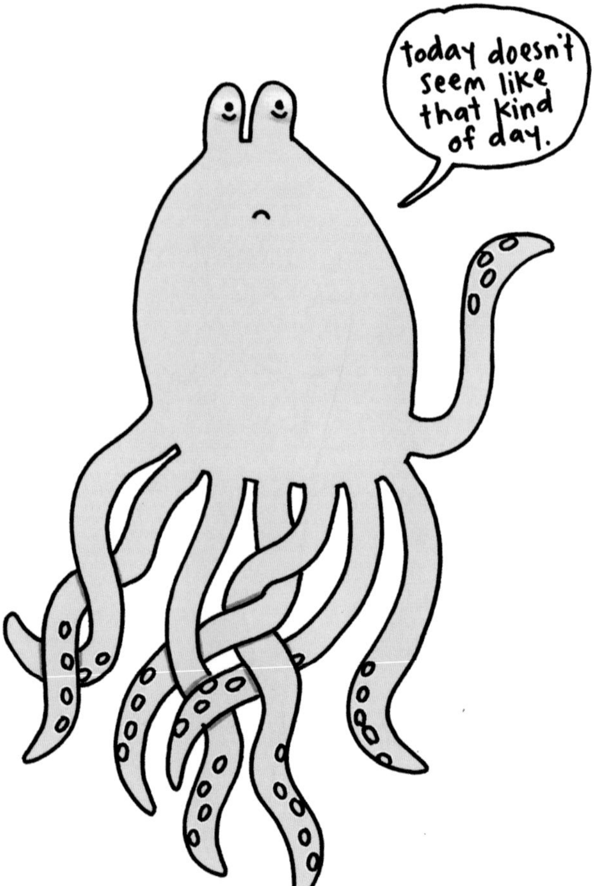
today doesn't seem like that kind of day.

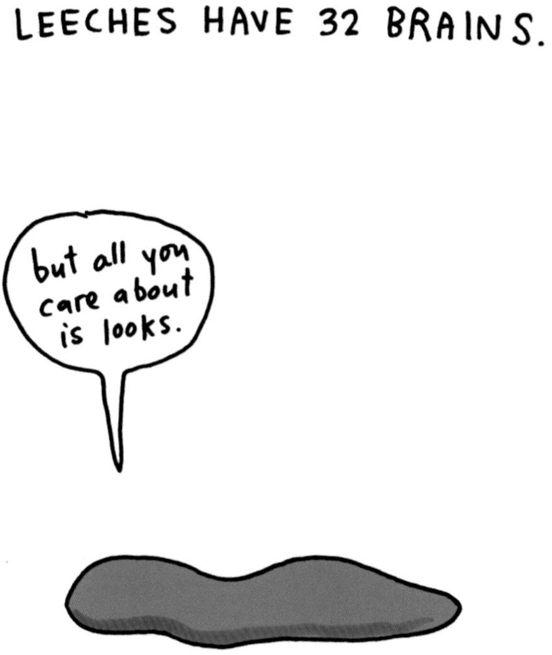
LEECHES HAVE 32 BRAINS.
but all you care about is looks.

A PORTUGUESE MAN O' WAR
IS ACTUALLY SEVERAL
ORGANISMS ATTACHED TOGETHER.

WHEN FLATWORMS ARE SLICED IN
HALF AND REGROW THEMSELVES
THEY HAVE THE SAME MEMORIES

it's a hard
thing to
forget.

IT TAKES A BANANA SLUG
24 HOURS TO GET SOMEWHERE
A BLOCK AWAY.

JELLYFISH HAVE NO HEARTS.

APPENDIX

Adélie penguins push each other off ledges to see if the water's safe. British explorer and Navy officer Robert Falcon Scott and his team observed Adélie penguins on their Antarctic expeditions in the early 1900's. One of his team members, George Murray Levick, described penguin bullies in his journal:

At the place where they most often went in [the water], a long terrace of ice about six feet in height ran for some hundreds of yards along the edge of the water, and here, just as on the sea-ice, crowds would stand near the brink. When they had succeeded in pushing one of their number over, all would crane their necks over the edge, and when they saw the pioneer safe in the water, the rest followed.

An albatross can pick up smells 12 miles away. Scientists once assumed that birds had a very poor sense of smell. Thank goodness for zoologist Gabrielle Nevitt, who in 1991 brought hundreds of boxes of tampons to Antarctica, dipped them in fish-scented liquid, and attached them to kites. Seabirds were immediately drawn to the smell and Nevitt's research prompted more investigation into birds' olfactory abilities. We now know that albatrosses fly in zigzag patterns covering thousands of square miles of ocean and use their incredible sense of smell to find their favorite food: rotting fish floating on the surface of the water.

An alligator's brain weighs less than an Oreo. The average alligator weighs 400 pounds but its brain weighs only 8 or 9 grams. The average Oreo weighs 12 grams. And that's only the original cookie—a Double Stuf Oreo weighs as much as three alligator brains. A Double Stuf Oreo is way too complex an idea for an alligator to process.

Ants don't sleep but they take 8-minute naps twice a day. Scientists aren't sure if ants really sleep at all, but they definitely do take naps. Research done on ants in 1930 and in 1986 found that ants rest for 8 minutes twice in a 24-hour period, and a 2009 study of a fire ant colony found that the ants took 250 one-minute naps in a 24-hour period. All the ants continued to work while they were asleep, no matter how long the nap was, so they're not getting too much rest.

Anteaters can be as big as humans, but the inside of their mouth is the size of an olive. Giant anteaters have to visit up to 200 anthills a day to get enough calories.

Apes tell lies. Koko is a 280-pound gorilla best known for her ability to communicate using sign language and her knowledge of over 1,000 signs. She lives in California with her trainer, Francine Patterson, and her pet kittens. Once, when researchers arrived at Koko's habitat, they found a sink had been ripped from a wall. Koko signed that one of the kittens was responsible for the damage. Sadly, kittens aren't strong enough to rip sinks from walls.

Aracari sleep with their heads in their armpits. Aracari are a type of toucan, and for reasons we don't understand, all toucans sleep in this position. One explanation is that tucking their bill under their wing keeps them from losing too much heat at night, sort of like wearing socks to bed.

Armadillos can't keep themselves warm and form groups when the temperature drops. Armadillos spend most of their lives alone. The only time they widen their social circle is in colder temperatures when they huddle together in small underground burrows.

Bald eagles save everything they find until their nests fall to the ground because the trees can't support their weight. Bald eagle couples work on their nests their whole lives, adding to them in the winter and guarding them in the summer. The nests grow bigger and bigger; the largest nest ever found was 9 feet across and 20 feet tall, and weighed 4,000 pounds.

It takes a banana slug 24 hours to get somewhere a block away. The average recorded speed of a banana slug ranges between 2.5 and 6.6 inches per minute, which is 300 to 792 feet in a 24-hour period. The size of a city block also varies, but most are between 300 and 500 feet.

Barn owls are usually monogamous but 25% of couples separate. Barn owls mate for life and immediately begin adding to their family, laying an average of a dozen eggs each year. A 2014 study by Amélie Dreiss and Alexandre Roulin in Switzerland discovered that if an owl couple has a bad mating season and very few eggs hatch or survive, the couple will split and both will look for new owl partners.

Bats have long-distance relationships. Male bats and female bats live in identical communities but at different altitudes, and meet up only when it's time to mate. Males live in higher altitudes and females live in lower altitudes, near water.

Beavers need to chew constantly because their teeth never stop growing. Beavers rely on their teeth to cut branches, build dams and canals, and eat bark from birch, maple, and cottonwood trees. Their teeth grow continuously so that they can chew to their hearts' content without worrying about them wearing down. Since their teeth grow an average of 4 feet a year, if a beaver stopped chewing, its teeth could grow into its brains or get caught on things.

If bees made minimum wage, a jar of honey would cost $182,000. In an hour's trip, a single honeybee can carry 0.04 grams of nectar in her little nectar stomach, and that amount of nectar can be converted into 0.02 grams of honey. That's 25,000 hours of bee labor to fill a 500 gram jar of honey (about the size of those jars that are shaped like bears).

25,000 hours at $7.25 minimum wage is $181,250, and I rounded it up to $182,000 for a few paid sick days, a yearly bonus, and possibly some taxes. If you've ever eaten honey before, you've gotten an amazing deal.

Birds can't go to space because they need gravity to swallow. Mammals swallow by constricting muscles in the esophagus to pull food from the mouth to the stomach. Birds, however, don't have as complicated an esophagus and rely on gravity, tilting their beaks to the sky and letting the meal fall down to be digested, sometimes with help from gravel they also swallow.

A female black bear can hibernate for up to 8 months. For eight months a bear's heart rate slows and the hibernating bear stops eating, drinking, urinating, and defecating. After waking up, they ease into spring and spend two weeks slowly walking around, getting used to being outside and moving.

Black eagles watch their children fight to the death without intervening. Like many other animals, black eagles often have seasons where they give birth to more children than they can raise. They solve this problem by letting their offspring kill each other off.

Blobfish have no muscles. The blobfish's weird composition means it weighs a little less than water, and can float around the ocean without using up any energy. It eats by opening its mouth and swallowing whatever happens to float in.

Burrowing owls laugh when they're afraid. A burrowing owl's standard call is the hoot sound you expect from owls, but when they're frightened they let out a quick, high-pitched cackle. The cackle is supposed to mimic the sound of a rattlesnake, but it's unclear who that is supposed to scare.

Butterflies taste everything they walk on. Butterfly taste buds are on the bottom of their feet, so they can tell by standing on a leaf if it's worth eating. If the leaf is a good one they'll lay their eggs on it so that their caterpillars can enjoy it. Butterflies themselves don't eat leaves, because they don't have teeth, and can't chew.

Camels can drink 30 gallons of water in 15 minutes. Camels can travel about 100 miles without drinking any water, but when they do find water they drink as much of it as they can. Most people think camels store water in their humps, but that's not what camel humps are for. Their humps are just full of fat that they live off of when there's nothing else to eat.

Polydactyl cats have thumbs but they aren't opposable. Polydactism, a long word for extra fingers and toes, is most prevalent in cats. Thumb cats are common on ships because they're considered to be good luck at sea, but they still need help opening cat food and feline sea-sickness tins and other things that require opposable thumbs.

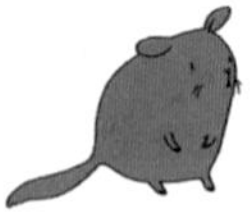

If a chinchilla gets wet, it might never dry. Chinchilla fur is so dense that it rarely dries on its own, and if it gets wet it can rot or develop a fungal infection. Pet chinchillas take dust baths to clean themselves, and in the wild, chinchillas bathe in volcanic ash.

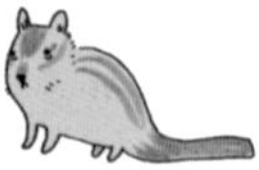

A chipmunk can't recognize its face in a mirror. Humans and a select group of animals can recognize their reflections in a mirror, which is a great skill. The mirror test is considered a sign of self-awareness, and is usually administered by putting a mark on the animal's face and observing to see if the animal inspects their face when they see their reflection. Chipmunks are clueless about their reflections.

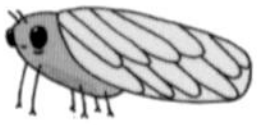

Cicadas stay underground for 17 years. Cicadas burrow underground and sleep for 17 years. They might feel rested after 10, 11, or 16 years, but coordinating their schedules means they can emerge en masse and lower their chances of being eaten by predators.

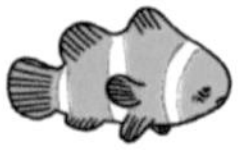

Clownfish have a slimy mucus coating. Clownfish live in colorful and incredibly toxic sea anemone that their predators avoid at all costs. Most clownfish are born with a sticky gelatinous coating that keeps them safe from the anemone stings. Some clownfish aren't born with the snot safety layer and have to acclimate by allowing themselves to be stung by the anemone over and over and over until they become immune.

The confusing thing is that even clownfish born with the protective coating repeatedly sting themselves, just to be safe.

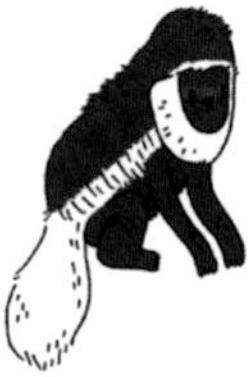

Colobus monkey stomachs can handle food that no one else will eat. A Colobus monkey's two- to four-part stomach (scientists still aren't sure) gives them more time to digest hard and unpalatable food that other animals would never try to eat, like delicious tree bark and unripened fruit.

Coot parents peck at their young if they ask for food, so only the quietest survive. A pair of coot parents could never care for all the eggs they lay, so they create a sort of game show.

The first chicks to hatch have an initial advantage, they get first dibs on food and never share with their unlucky younger siblings. Because of the extra food, the oldest chicks grow even faster.

After a week of this most of the younger coots die of starvation, and the mom and dad each pick one surviving youngest baby that they want to let live. They care for these starving chicks, and bite and shake the older ones if they ask for food. Because of the extra food, the favorite chicks now grow even faster, until the young favorites are bigger than their older siblings—if their older siblings are still alive.

Cougars can't roar but they can scream. Even though cougars are eight feet long, they're technically classified as small cats because of their vocal cords. Large cats have cartilage between their tongues and windpipes that allows them to make roaring noises while small cats can only hiss and meow. To compensate for this, female cougars scream to communicate with each other.

Cows produce the most milk when they listen to R.E.M.'s "Everybody Hurts." In 2001 two scientists at the University of Leicester studied which songs make cows produce the most milk. The cows responded best to very calming music. Relaxed cows produce more oxytocin, which makes them produce more milk.

City coyotes live longer than coyotes in the wilderness. The main cause of death of urban coyotes is collision with motor vehicles, and the main cause of death of rural coyotes is starvation or attack by predators.

Sections of highway on Christmas Island are closed for red crab migration. There are 10 to 40 million red crabs on Christmas Island, and all of them live in the forests. Around October of each year all 10 to 40 million red crabs head to the coasts to mate. The round-trip journey causes serious traffic problems, and after many crabs died and others punctured car tires, it was time to do something. Today some sections of highway are closed during crab season, and in other places small tunnels guide crabs under major roads. Because the red crabs live in the forest and reproduce on the beach, if something happened to them it would throw off both the forest ecosystem and the beach ecosystem.

Girl crickets can't chirp. Crickets chirp to attract mates, so apparently female crickets don't need to do it. Male crickets have leathery segments on their wings that create a chirping sound when rubbed together. Making noises by rubbing is called stridulation and female crickets are crazy about it. Males make an initial mating call when a female is nearby and they make a different, celebratory call after mating.

Crocodiles lived with dinosaurs. Crocodiles, along with alligators, frogs, and turtles, have been on earth for 180 million years, which is before dinosaurs existed. In 2015 the perfectly preserved remains of a 9-foot prehistoric crocodile were found in Bavaria.

Crows never forget a face. Crows will remember the face of someone they dislike for their entire lives, and will often enlist other crows in attacking the person.

In a 2011 study by the University of Washington, John Marzluff and other researchers wore two masks around forested areas in Washington: a caveman mask and a mask of former U.S. vice president Dick Cheney. Initially, neither mask elicited a reaction from the crows they encountered.

Then, while wearing the caveman mask, a member of the team captured several dozen crows and placed them in temporary crates. Once released, the birds spread the word and from that point on, researchers wearing the caveman masks were attacked by murders of crows. The crows recognized the caveman mask immediately based on a description they had heard from the captured crows, and hated the caveman even when the mask was worn upside down.

All the crows continued to ignore researchers wearing the Dick Cheney mask.

Dik diks mark their territory with their tears. Dik diks ooze sticky black "tears" from preorbital glands near their eyes. They rub these tears on plants to define their territory and let people know what a terrible time they're having on the savannas of eastern Africa.

Dogs can't see television, but they pretend to like it so they can be close to you. Human televisions are designed for human eyes and brains, and show us just enough frames per second to trick us into seeing a moving image. To the wrong sort of brain, television just looks like a slideshow, which isn't that interesting to dogs. The great news is that modern televisions have sped up enough that dogs can watch television with you while they sit next to you on the couch. Experts claim dogs won't truly enjoy television until it involves more smell, but that seems like a lot to ask.

Two dogs were hanged for witchcraft during the Salem witch trials. During the Salem witch trials, 19 humans were killed as convicted witches and 2 dogs were killed after it was suggested that they were the witches' accomplices. At the time, a popular method of detecting witches involved baking urine from possibly possessed humans into small cakes and feeding the cakes to dogs to see if anything happened.

Only half a dolphin's brain sleeps at a time. Because dolphins can't breathe underwater, they can't sleep underwater without drowning. Instead, only half of a dolphin's brain sleeps at a time. While the left half sleeps, the right half stays awake and focuses on breathing and all the other things dolphin thinks about. To add to the confusion, the sleeping side of the dolphin keeps its eye open while the awake side closes its eye.

Dragonfly migration takes 4 generations. Dragonfly migration happens on every continent except Antarctica and many species of dragonflies cross numerous countries and oceans to get between their summer and winter homes. Though one dragonfly might not live to complete its migration, their offspring knows to continue in the direction their ancestors were traveling in order to eventually complete the cycle.

Anything a duckling meets within 10 minutes of being born becomes its parent. Animals that hatch usually assume the first moving object they see is their parent. This phenomenon is called imprinting and allows them to immediately form a bond so they can start learning important survival skills. Ducklings have been known to imprint themselves to rain boots, trains, or anything else that happens to be nearby. Since having a rain boot for a mother can be scary and strange, researchers raising ducklings in captivity often interact with the recent hatchlings using a duck puppet.

Dwarf lemurs line their homes with feces. Dwarf lemurs sleep curled up in small and terrible-smelling holes in trees.

Elephants can't jump. Because of their weight, it's difficult for adult elephants to lift more than one leg off the ground at a time, and it's impossible for them to jump. Baby elephants have an easier time jumping, and elephants of all ages are amazing swimmers.

Elephant babies suck on their trunks the way human babies suck on their thumbs. Just like humans, baby elephants are born with an instinct to suck on things, and they will usually continue to suck on their trunk to calm themselves until they get a little older. Sometimes older elephants will suck their trunks for some comfort when they are upset.

In crowded groups of emperor penguins, mates find each other by smell instead of sight. Penguins live in large groups, and being familiar with their mate's smell (and the smell of their friends and other family members) makes it easier and faster to find them and their nest after everyone gets back from swimming.

Emus can't walk backward. Emus are incredibly fast when moving forward, but rarely take steps backward. Because of this, the flightless bird is featured on the Australian coat of arms, along with the kangaroo, and the motto "Advance Australia."

Fennec fox ears take up a third of their body. The fennec fox may be the smallest species of fox, but it has six-inch-long ears. Blood vessels in fennec fox ears radiate extra heat, keeping the foxes cool in their Saharan habitat. The foxes also have extra-sensitive hearing, and can even hear sounds underground if they want to.

If a female ferret goes into heat and doesn't mate she will die. People like to neuter male ferrets because it reduces their smell. People like to neuter female ferrets because if female ferrets are not neutered and they go into heat, they'll stay in heat forever until the high levels of estrogen lead to aplastic anemia, and they die from severe anemia or bacterial infections.

Adult fireflies don't eat. Most adult fireflies feed off food they ate when they were larvae. The only exception is the Photuris firefly, which eats other adult fireflies after attracting them with a glowing mating signal.

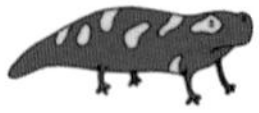

Fire salamanders eat their siblings. Fire salamanders would like to eat small fish and insects but will resort to whatever they have to. If resources are scarce, they will eat other species of salamanders, and if resources are scarce and they're really in a hurry, they'll resort to their own family members.

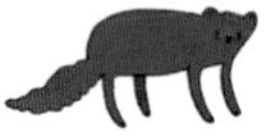

A female fisher can be pregnant for 350 days in a year. Female fishers mate in late March, and deliver their babies in early March of the next year. They then wait another week before becoming pregnant again.

Scientists don't understand why flamingos stand on one leg. Flamingo legs are longer than their bodies, which should make standing on one leg difficult, but for some reason they do it for hours a day. Here are five popular theories:

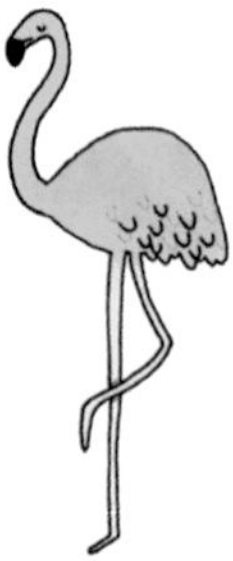

1. Flamingos might be taking advantage of unihemispheric sleeping, where one half of the body sleeps at a time, and the lifted leg is taking a break.
2. Pulling one leg closer to the body could make it easier to pump blood to it, and could heat the body faster.
3. Putting your legs in a pool of cold water makes you lose heat pretty quickly, so standing on one leg could be a way around that.
4. The standing leg could be more prone to getting water funguses or parasites.
5. Finally, the position could be an attempt to camouflage flamingos to underwater creatures they want to eat. From underwater one flamingo leg might look like a reed, and two legs just looks like some sort of two-legged animal. This theory is not great, since most of the things flamingoes eat have very poor eyesight. Or maybe that makes the theory even better, since they're very easily fooled.

When flatworms are sliced in half and regrow themselves they have the same memories. Flatworms are know for their ability to regenerate and can do so because each of their cells can become any cell in their body. Flatworms also hate bright lights. In one notable flatworm study, a team put a delicious piece of liver in a bright room and coaxed the worms to go into the light to eat it. Eventually they learned to deal with the light and go into the bright area to find the food.

 Then the researchers cut off the worms' heads. Once the flatworms regrew their heads, they headed straight toward the bright light to claim their liver, remembering the previous experience despite their beheadings.

In another study, researchers trained flatworms to find their way through a maze, then rewarded them by grinding them up and feeding them to other flatworms. The flatworms who had just eaten the maze-experts seemed to be pretty good at figuring out the maze, even though they had never seen it before.

 Foxes live, work, eat, and sleep alone. Other animals hunt together and clean each other and curl up in a hole to snuggle at night, but a fox sleeps outdoors alone with its tail covering its face. Foxes pair up only to mate and raise their young before sending them off to live alone.

 Frogs can close their ears. Frogs live in noisy swamps, so they wouldn't be able to hear each other if they didn't have the ability to isolate and tune out some frequencies of sound. Different species of frogs listen to different frequencies, so it's possible for two frogs in the same pond to not be able to hear each other.

 Garden lizards eat their own tails for calcium. Some lizards have a defense mechanism called autonomy, which means they can detach their tail. Lizards like this usually have very brightly colored tails so they're the first thing a predator wants to check out, allowing the lizard a quick and tail-less escape. Garden lizards have this ability, and the only time it causes problems is when a pet lizard in captivity becomes stressed out and detaches its own tail for no good reason. The missing tail contains a lot of calcium, so when it seems safe to do so lizards will sometimes circle back to it and eat it.

Gibbon calls can be heard 2 miles away. Gibbons are crazy about singing. Male and female pairs often perform duets together, singing slightly different notes to harmonize. Different species of gibbons have similar coloring, but are identified by their different songs. If you like gibbon calls you're in luck, they are incredibly loud and can be heard from a great distance. If you don't like gibbon calls, that makes sense, because they sound like car alarms.

Giraffe sleep 3 hours a night. Giraffes sleep between 1.9 and 4.6 hours a night, depending on whether they're in the wild or in captivity.

Giraffe babies fall six feet to the ground when they're born. Giraffes give birth standing up, which means a baby giraffe's first encounter with the world is getting hit in the face by it. Newborn giraffes are about six feet tall and can stand up an hour after they're born.

All gnu are born during a 3-week period. Gnu (or wildebeest) are migratory animals and spend their entire life on the move. To make this possible, the pack syncs the mating season so that all the young are born and raised quickly.

Goats can see almost 360 degrees around them. Goat eyes have rectangular pupils, which give them a wider field of vision. I found a website called Goat Simulator that I hoped would explain this more (is it like a fisheye lens?) but the website is just reviews of an incredibly violent video game where you are a goat.

The average goldcrest lives 8 months. The average goldcrest lives eight months, with some dying very early and some living long enough to reproduce and create more goldcrests that also won't live very long.

Gorillas can catch human colds. Gorillas share over 98 percent of genetic material with humans, and we share a lot of germs too. Sick gorillas exhibit the same symptoms as humans: runny nose, coughing, sneezing, and exhaustion. Gorillas in the wild can also catch viruses from human tourists, and these colds are more likely to spread and lead to animal fatalities. Gorillas in captivity are more likely to get flu shots.

Guinea pigs sleep with their eyes open. Some guinea pigs close their eyes to sleep when they feel incredibly safe, but it's not common. If you own a guinea pig and it stares into space a lot, it might be sleeping.

Guppies can't take naps because they don't have eyelids. If you leave the light on in the room your guppy sleeps it will be completely miserable.

Hammerhead sharks can smell electricity. Sharks and other large underwater animals have "ampullae of Lorenzini," jelly-like electrorecepting organs that help them detect electric fields in the water they swim in. All living things produce a slight electrical field and sharks are more sensitive to these electric fields than any other animal. This helps them detect prey even if it's hiding in darkness or under sand. The shape of a hammerhead shark's head might help them sense electricity even better, or it might just be shaped that way because they think it looks good.

Guacamole is extremely poisonous to hamsters. Avocados contain persin, a toxin that is harmful to almost all animals. When persin is eaten by any nonhuman creature it can cause vomiting and diarrhea and possibly death. Persin is found only in avocados.

Before you get any ideas, here are other foods hamsters can't eat: apple seeds, eggplant, elderberries, mushrooms, peppers, garlic, onions, beans, raisins, potatoes, tomatoes, almonds, peanuts, all citrus fruits, chocolate, and high-fat meat.

Harp seal pups are abandoned on beaches at birth, and 30% don't survive. Harp seal parents give birth to one pup a year, a snow white baby seal that they set on packed ice. The parents care for the seal for a little over a week, until they lose interest and abandon it on the ice forever.

Unlike other animals left on beaches at birth, harp seals cannot walk or swim or fend for themselves until they are 8 weeks old, which gives them 45 terrifying days to starve to death or be eaten by wandering polar bears. The baby seals will usually cry for their parents for a while after they leave, then stop making noise or moving, to conserve their energy and not call any attention to themselves from predators. Baby seals that survive lose 50 percent of their body weight during this period.

Herrings communicate with farts. Herrings have excellent hearing. Instead of vocalizing to communicate with each other, they're able to fart and listen to the bubbles other herrings create in the water.

Groundhog day was hedgehog day until the 1800s. This shadow-based holiday originated with a Candlemas custom in Germany, when festive people would test the weather by looking at a hedgehog's shadow and reciting this catchy poem:

If Candlemas day be dry and fair,
The half o' winter to come and mair,
If Candlemas day be wet and foul,
The half of winter's gone at Yule.

When German settlers arrived in Pennsylvania there were no hedgehogs to be seen, so they substituted a groundhog for the hedgehog.

Hippos attract mates by peeing. Hippos use their pee for almost everything, from dominant territory marking to submissive peeing.

Hornbill chicks come out of the nest when they're a few days old, then immediately go back in for another few months. Hornbill reproduction is incredibly complicated and starts with prospective hornbill parents finding a tree with a hollow trunk. When she's ready to lay the eggs, the female hornbill goes in the small space in the tree and the male uses sap and mud to seal off the entrance and trap her safely inside. He leaves a small opening big enough to push snacks through, and spends a few weeks looking for fruit, nuts, and meat to bring her as she lays her eggs and incubates them. The female loses many of her feathers to make herself smaller so that she and the newborns can fit in the tree trunk together once they hatch. The mother and babies stay in the small tree hollow and the father continues bringing them nourishment for a few more days. Eventually the mother knocks down the wall and breaks out, and the chicks rebuild the wall using wall remnants and their own feces, and stay inside for several more weeks. Sometimes their parents help seal them back in, sometimes the offspring do it on their own.

Horses that look like they're smiling are actually smelling the air. This is called the flehmen response, and is a way of holding the mouth and tongue so that smells move quickly to the nose to be inspected for anything interesting. It looks like a laugh or a grin and is also common in deer and big cats. When housecats use the flehmen response it looks more like a disgusted grimace. The word comes from the German word flehmen, which means to show the teeth.

Houseflies can only hum in the key of F. Housefly hums are caused by wing vibration and the frequency of their wing flaps determines the pitch. Since their wings only beat at one frequency, there's only one sound they can make.

If humans had the metabolism of hummingbirds they'd have to eat 400 hamburgers a day. A human-sized hummingbird would consume energy 10 times faster than an Olympic marathon runner. The average hamburger contains over 350 calories, and 400 hamburgers adds up to 140,000 calories, over 2 months of calories for the average human. Hummingbirds are able to start using their calories before they even convert them into anything, which saves them some energy.

Hyacinth macaws have the intelligence of a 3-year-old. Hyacinth macaws can be trained to solve puzzles and find objects.

Hyenas eat rotting meat. Hyenas eat carrion (the scientific word for rotting meat) without getting sick because their stomachs have more acidity that kills the bacteria.

Hyraxes have 30 different calls. Rock hyraxes sing long songs to communicate, made up of a variety of calls. Different dialects exist in different communities of rock hyraxes throughout Africa and the Middle East.

Jellyfish have no hearts. Jellyfish don't have hearts, or stomachs, or many other things most organisms have. Some jellyfish can live forever, which means the ocean might always be filled with heartless jellyfish just swimming around not caring about anyone.

Kangaroos cough to show submission. If a kangaroo approaches you and seems aggressive, experts recommend coughing slowly and loudly as you crawl away in fear.

Kiwis can remember a bad memory for 5 years. Dr. Hugh Robertson placed tape recorders with kiwi calls (male calls sound like cute whistles and female calls sound like screams) around areas where kiwis lived. The birds were tricked by the fake kiwi calls, went to investigate them, and were captured. But only once. After they were released the kiwis didn't take any chances, avoiding—for the next five years—the specific areas where the recordings had been.

Koalas are only social for 15 minutes a day. Koalas have a terribly inefficient metabolism and have to spend almost all of their time eating to get energy, or sleeping to conserve energy. This leaves a total of 15 minutes of quality time during the day to groom and chat about whatever koalas chat about.

Koi fish can live 200 years. The average koi life span is 25 to 35 years but many live past 200. There are lots of anecdotal stories about koi fish living almost forever, but the oldest documented koi fish died in 1977 at the age of 226. Her name was Hanako.

Leeches have 32 brains. Believe it or not, leech genetic makeup is very different from humans. Their 32 brains are sort of like one long brain divided up into 32 different ganglia, or groups of nerve cells. Leeches also have mouths at both ends of their bodies and teeth on the outside of their mouths.

Male lions eat first and make the women and children eat last. Although female lions do the hunting, male lions eat first and everyone else watches them eat and waits until they're finished.

Little brown bats are awake for 4 hours a day. Little brown bats in captivity sleep for almost 20 hours every day, and conserve almost all their energy for a short bug-hunting sprint.

When early ocean explorers thought they saw mermaids they were actually looking at manatees. Rumors of half-fish half-human beings that attract sailors, steal their gold, and drag them to the bottom of the sea have been around for 1,900 years, and they were and still are often depicted in stories and in art. So Columbus was excited to see some in person near the Dominican Republic in 1493. He described them as "not half as beautiful as they are painted." Manatees are 9-foot 1,000-pound slow-moving aquatic mammals that may be an ancient relative of the elephant. Manatees have no natural predators; their unnatural predator is boats.

A Portuguese man o' war is actually several organisms attached together. Many people mistake this thing for a jellyfish, but a Portuguese man o' war is a siphonophore—that is, a colony of many animals connected and working together and acting as one organism.

15 mara families live in one burrow. Mara are larger relatives of the guinea pig that live in South America. In mara burrows, one adult will stay behind to look after everyone's young at once, while the other adults go out and look for food or do whatever else they want to do.

Marine iguanas sneeze out salt when they eat too much of it. A marine iguana's diet consists completely of underwater algae that it scrapes off rocks with its teeth. The algae and water and everything around them is incredibly salty, and the tops of their heads turn white from the crusted salt they sneeze out.

The average mayfly lives less than a day. The last stage of a mayfly's life is very short, and adults don't eat or drink and are filled with air.

Meerkat babies are given dead scorpions to play with. Meerkats are immune to scorpion venom, and eat scorpions as well as plants and insects. Parents begin teaching their young how to hunt scorpions at an early age, and mostly by example.

Mice can sense sadness in other mice and it makes them sad too. A team of researchers gave mice a slight stomachache and put them in a space with another mouse who did not have a stomachache. When the stomachache mouse tensed in discomfort, the other mouse would feel it too and tense also. The empathy was stronger if the two mice had previously lived in the same cage together.

Monk seals can't dream underwater. Unihemispheric sleep allows seals to put half of their brain to sleep at a time, so they can swim while sleeping, but REM can't happen during this type of sleep. Seals can also rest on the shore to sleep. When seals do dream, I don't know what they dream about, but if you ever have a dream about a seal it could be a sign that a good business deal is coming up, or it could mean you miss your family, or it could symbolize a wedding (if it is a white seal).

Moose eat for 8 hours a day. Moose don't engage in too many activities besides grazing, and eat up to 60 pounds of leaves a day.

Mosquitofish can only count to 100. Mosquitofish are social creatures and their goal is to be with as many other fish as possible. In one study researchers showed fish different doors with different numbers of shapes on them, and more shapes meant more fish were behind the door. When the difference between the numbers was 2:3 (if one door had 8 shapes 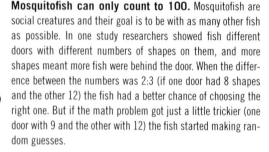 and the other 12) the fish had a better chance of choosing the right one. But if the math problem got just a little trickier (one door with 9 and the other with 12) the fish started making random guesses.

The scientists performed the same test on humans (without the swimming and doors and rooms full of fish, they just gave them a computer test) and saw the same results.

 Moths have no stomachs. Moths don't have anything like our stomachs, but they have a system that works well and involves a midgut and a gizzard.

 Narwhal means "corpse whale" because of their blotchy, translucent skin. In Norse, "nar" means corpse and "hval" means whale, because their spotted bloated skin looks like a drowned sailor.

Nurse sharks lose a tooth a week. Sharks can have up to 3,000 teeth at a time, arranged in 5 rows. The front row of teeth are the biggest and work the hardest at tearing food up, and subsequent rows are smaller and replace the front row as they fall out. Teeth wear out faster in the summer because that's when sharks eat the most frequently. In a shark's lifetime it will go through 35,000 teeth.

An octopus lives alone and leaves home only when necessary. Octopi live alone in small octopus-sized dens on the ocean floor. These dens are usually spaces under rocks, but octopi have also been known to hide away inside jars and bottles if they find them. They leave only to hunt for food.

Opossum moms carry their children on their backs. Opossums have up to 20 children at a time, which start out the size of a human thumb and live in her pouch. As they grow older and bigger and heavier they ride on her back as she searches for food for them.

An ostrich spends 7 months alone every year. Colder months are very lonely for ostriches, but they spend the summer in groups of about 30 birds and other roaming animals like zebras and antelopes.

Owls can't move their eyes because they don't have eyeballs, they have eye tubes. Owl eyes are advanced to help them see at great distances and in very low light. Part of this adaptation includes "sclerotic rings" that attach to the back of the eye and hold it to the owl's head; this limits the owl's ability to move its eyes around. Their eyes also have a much narrower field of vision than humans and other birds, before eye motion is involved.

Pandas don't have set sleeping areas, they just fall asleep wherever they are. A giant panda's daily 12 hours of sleep doesn't happen in a designated place, just wherever they happen to be when the mood strikes them.

Male white front parrots vomit on females they want to mate with. White front parrots are one of the only known animals that engage in mouth-to-mouth kissing. Unfortunately, their kissing ends with the male vomiting into the female's mouth.

Male peacocks make fake mating sounds to attract females. Peacock mating involves a loud, very specific shriek that males make just before mating. Often male peacocks will make this sound alone, for no reason, when female peacocks aren't close by but may be within earshot. Scientists at Duke University believe these fake mating calls make females believe that a male is more popular than he actually is.

Pigs have trouble seeing the sky because of how their eyes are placed. Possibly not true, need to talk to farmer.

Pigeons put off things they don't want to do. In a 2011 study pigeons were taught how to peck at a small disk to dispense food. They could either peck 8 times, or wait 15 seconds and then have to peck 35 to 40 times. Other similar studies have been done on pigeons with the same results, the pigeons will always wait as long as possible before completing the task, even if waiting means they have to do much more work later. Pigeons are popular subjects for procrastination tests because they're very fast learners and also very impatient.

Pit vipers have heat sensors on their mouths. The heat sensors help pit vipers see heat, so they can find lunch even if they'll never find love.

A platypus swims with its eyes closed. A platypus's face has a fold of skin that covers its eyes and ears. When underwater, the platypus covers its eyes to keep water out and feels around for food using its bill.

Strawberry poison dart frogs feed their unfertilized eggs to their hatched babies. The 2 months that strawberry poison dart frog couples spend caring for their young make them some of the most attentive amphibian parents. The females lay eggs in groups of 5. The first 5 eggs grow into tadpoles, and all the eggs the female lays after that are fed to her tadpoles.

Pregnant polar bears gain 500 pounds. The average female polar bear weighs 331 to 550 pounds, and pregnant polar bears can weigh up to 1,100 pounds.

Newborn porcupines are ready to injure someone within minutes of being born. Porcupine is Latin for "quill pig," and one may have up to 30,000 quills. Their quills can grow up to a foot long and they grow new ones to replace the ones they stick in enemies. Babies are born with soft quills that quickly start to harden.

Prairie dogs have different calls to communicate different human heights and human shirt colors but can't differentiate between circles and squares. Dr. Con Slobodchikoff spent 30 blissful years researching prairie dogs in the wild. Prairie dogs live together in underground burrows and make alarm calls to each other when predators are near. To the untrained ear the calls sound like chirps, but subtle differences actually communicate different types of threats (hawk, bus, human) and even include details like weight and shirt color. Slobodchikoff can now identify the different calls just by listening.

Puma, mountain lions, and cougars are all the same animal. This 6- to 8-foot large cat is also called the Florida panther, catamount, wildcat, silver lion, and over 40 other names, and it holds the Guinness world record for having more names than any other animal. Because the animal is found in so many places and so many countries across North, Central, and South America, it's been given different names by different cultures.

Boy puppies let girl puppies win when they playfight.
When male puppies playfight with female puppies they go to
extreme lengths to make sure the females win; putting themselves in vulnerable positions and celebrating playfully when

they're defeated. Some researchers say that since female puppies don't usually like fighting with males (female fighting is
vicious later on so females need all the practice they can get)
the male dogs might be trying to make themselves more fun
and a more appealing playfighting opponent. Other researchers
say the males probably just have a crush on the females, but
my teacher said the same thing when a boy bit my arm in kin-
dergarten, and I still think she was wrong.

**Domesticated rabbits live 8 years as pets or 24 hours
on their own.** There are so many wild rabbits living just outside your home that it might seem like a great idea to set your

pet rabbit free in a nearby park. The bad news is that rabbits,
both domestic and wild, need a safe place to hide in case of
danger. In your house a rabbit might sprint under a specific
dresser, in the wild a rabbit might sprint to a burrow, but most
pet rabbits set free outside don't survive the night because they
don't have time to find a safe place before it's too late.

**Raccoon hands are nimble enough to steal a dime
from your shirt pocket.** Raccoons have amazing hands that
allow them to casually climb down trees face first, as well as
open jars, turn doorknobs, unlatch latches, and take care of any
loose change you're trying to get rid of.

**The ring-tailed lemur that smells the worst is in charge
of the whole group.** Lemurs use smell for almost everything,
and even cut into trees around their home to embed the bark
with their scent. The female lemur with the strongest smell is in
charge of the pack, but males smell bad in their own way. Male
ring-tailed lemurs have small scent glands on their shoulders
that ooze a sticky brown horrible-smelling paste. They use their

tails to fling this paste at each other during stink fights, which can last up to an hour.

 Lab rats enjoy mating more when they're wearing vests. Lucky researchers at the University of Montreal found young rats who were inexperienced in the ways of the world, put tiny little vests on them, and encouraged them to mate. The team repeated these steps with the same rats a few times until the males were used to the vests. They then took half the vests away, and when all the rats were again encouraged to mate, the little guys without their vests were less interested.

 **Red ruffed lemurs leave their kids when they go look for food.** These lemurs give birth to 2-6 little lemurs at once and build them a nest high in the trees of Madagascar, where their fathers look after them. Sixty-five percent of red ruffed lemurs don't make it past 3 months because they are taken by predators or fall from the trees.

 Rhinos make a squeaking sound to call for their friends when they're lost. Rhinos can make a variety of different sounds but the saddest is a loud squeak they use to look for each other.

 Roadrunners make themselves cry to get rid of excess salt. Roadrunners can run 20 miles an hour, are excellent hunters, and can eat both meat and vegetation. It may seem like they have great lives and never cry, but the opposite is true. The salty tears they cry reduce the salt in their blood.

 Scorpions are nocturnal hunters but they glow in the dark. The moon's UV light makes scorpions turn bright fluorescent blue and researchers aren't sure why, especially since the glow scares away things scorpions want to eat. The best time to find scorpions is under a full moon. (Or the worst time, if you don't like seeing glowing scorpions.)

Sea otters live in almost-freezing water that would kill a human in an hour. Sea otters stay alive in super unpleasant circumstances by having the densest hair ever—every square inch of their body has as many hairs as an entire human head. The saltiness of seawater makes it freeze at a lower temperature, so the water sea otters swim in can actually be below freezing. They're very serious about all the hair they have, and spend hours slowly and carefully grooming themselves to trap tiny bubbles as an extra layer of insulation.

Sea turtles never meet their moms. A prospective sea turtle mother will crawl awkwardly onto the sand, use a snow-angel-like motion to dig a shallow hole, and then lay about 100 eggs. After she does she will leave and never look back. The babies bite their way out of the eggs and crawl awkwardly to the ocean. Never really recovering from their lonely and traumatic beach experience, they like to spend time alone, and you'll almost never see two sea turtles together.

Great Britain has invested hundreds of thousands of pounds to study why seagulls attack so many people at outdoor festivals. Seagull attacks are a serious problem in many areas around Great Britain, so much so that Prime Minister David Cameron announced that "a big conversation needs to happen." Aside from ruining a festival, aggressive seagulls have also attacked a security guard, a swan in a public park, a Yorkshire terrier, and a Chihuahua puppy.

Seahorses are one of the only animals where the males become pregnant. Male seahorses get eggs from their mates and seal them up in a pouch. The expectant fathers change color when they're ready to give birth, and labor can last twelve hours. One great thing about males giving birth is it allows the couple to have children faster, since the female can be making more eggs while the male is carrying and giving birth to the last batch. A male can give birth to a thousand babies and get pregnant again in the same day. Seahorse couples mate for life and don't care for their young once they're born.

Shark pregnancies can last years. The spiny dogfish shark has a great name but a terrible length of pregnancy; its gestation lasts 24 months. Since this type of shark is ovoviviparous (the black diamond of hangman words) she lays eggs that hatch inside her body, and the baby shark continues to grow inside her until it's ready to be born.

Sheep can only remember 50 faces. In this study, a team of neuroscientists in England put up two doors on a barn, and displayed a life-sized sheep face on each door. One face always had food behind it and the sheep learned to seek out that specific face. Since sheep and humans use the same type of brain activity to recall a face, it's possible that sheep might remember and think about a favorite face when they haven't seen it in a while.

Long-tailed skinks eat their own eggs. If a skink lays her eggs in a place surrounded by predators she won't waste any time eating them. She'd rather have her children be her lunch than someone else's, and she needs the nutrients so she can lay more eggs, which she might also eat. You get it.

Sloths come down from their trees once a week to use the bathroom. Scientists are very curious about sloth poop. Get in line, scientists! These very slow animals spend all of their lives in trees except for the once-a-week descents to handle their business. Going to the ground is dangerous as it exposes them to predators, and no one knows for sure why they need to make the journey instead of just relieving themselves from trees.

If you cut off a snail's eye, it will grow back. The reason we know snail's eyes grow back is stranger than I could have ever possibly imagined, and I'm assuming it's stranger than you could have ever possibly imagined. A parasite called a leucochloriium paradoxum (green-banded broodsac for short) infects snails' eyes and make them swell up and pulse in bright green, red, and yellow stripes. The snails look like slow-moving neon signs and you really should look for a video of it. The parasite's goal is for these glowing, waving stripes to attract birds, which swoop down and eat off the snails' delicious infected eyes. The birds digest the whole mess and the leucochloriium paradoxum end up in the bird poop, which the snails eat, continuing the bizarre cycle. So, if you cut off a snail's eye its eye will grow back. And if you put a glowing parasite into a snail's eye that makes a bird eat its eye, its eye will also grow back.

Snow leopards eat 20 pounds of food a night. A snow leopard can catch an animal three times its own weight. They hunt mostly sheep and ibexes that weigh less than they do, and usually catch one animal a week and spend the rest of the week slowly eating it.

A sparrow will eat anything that fits into its mouth. House sparrows are an invasive species in North America, where their varied diet and street smarts make them a threat to other birds. Their favorite food is millet, but they also eat grain, moths, caterpillars, grass, leaves, and will scavenge trash cans for leftover food when they can.

Some species of spiders eat through their mom when they're born. The last thing these unlucky mother spiders experience is hundreds of babies chewing through them and into the world.

Squirrels can't burp. Squirrels can't burp or vomit, and they also can't have heartburn.

When star tortoise eggs hatch at cold temperatures more males are born, and when they hatch at warm temperatures more females are born. The best temperature for star tortoise egg incubation is around 85 degrees Fahrenheit, and lower or higher temperatures lead to a group of mostly males or mostly females. As soon as I thought about how interesting it would be if humans were like this I couldn't stop thinking about it for days.

Tarantulas can go years without eating. Tarantulas live up to 20 years and, anecdotally, can survive 2 years on water alone if they absolutely have to. In the wild tarantulas take their sweet time hunting crickets, grasshoppers, and sometimes even bats, frogs, and mice. Several disheartened Yahoo Answers contributors say they have learned the hard way that their pet tarantula can't go more than a month without food.

Tarsier eyes are bigger than their stomachs. Each of a tarsier's eyeballs is over half an inch in diameter, which may not seem huge but is bigger than its brain and bigger than its stomach. They use their enormous eyes to look for small things to eat in pitch darkness.

After Tasmanian devils mate, the female sneaks away in the night. Tasmanian devil mating is out of control and would make for reality television I would definitely be interested in watching at least once. A female Tasmanian devil wants the strongest and most aggressive male. She'll make a call to attract potential guys: If one is too timid she'll beat him up, but if one is strong and bites and scratches her, they'll mate. After mating, the male falls asleep and the female tries ever so secretly to move slowly out of the den so she can go mate with another male while she's still in heat. If the male wakes up he'll try to drag her back, and they'll fight some more. A lot of screaming is involved. If she sneaks away or wins the fight she'll go find another partner—a litter of Tasmanian devils from one mother can have up to four fathers.

Tigers don't like making eye contact while they hunt. Because tigers prefer sneak attacks, they usually don't look into their prey's eyes. Some people suggest making eye contact with a tiger if it's trying to attack you, but none of those people have been attacked by tigers so it's hard to say for sure if it's good advice.

Turtles breathe out their butts. Turtles can breathe out their mouths as well, but why bother when you can breathe out your butt instead? To observe this, scientists put small, safe amounts of coloring in water near turtles and observed them pulling oxygen from the colored water. This type of breathing uses fewer muscles and lets the turtles conserve less energy in the winter.

Walruses breathe on the ocean floor to uncover food hidden in the sand. The foods walruses like best are clams and shellfish that they discover by feeling around on the ocean floor until they find something they think is interesting.

Water-holding frogs eat their own skin for nutrients. Water-holding frogs live in Australia, and during very hot and dry periods they bury themselves underground and eat their skin for nourishment.

Baby whales gain 200 pounds a day. A newborn blue whale is 25 feet long and weighs 6,000 pounds. And even though they eat only tiny krill, they grow up to be 100 feet long and weigh 400,000 pounds.

Whales that sing in the wrong key get lost and are alone in the ocean. A lonely baleen whale discovered in 1989 in the north Pacific sings at a much higher frequency than other whales, so much higher that other whales aren't able to detect her song. She also travels along a different migration path ruining her chances of running into anyone just by accident. Her frequency, 52 Hertz, is about the pitch of a tuba, if that helps you imagine.

Wild yaks eat snow to stay hydrated. Yaks do best at higher altitudes, and become sick from heat in temperatures over 60 degrees Fahrenheit. Their favorite temperature is cold and their favorite way to get water is snow.

If a wolf is kicked out of its pack it never howls again. Wolf howls can be initiated by any member of the pack, and as soon as it's started the whole group joins in. Howls can be used to defend their space, call for someone, or just sort of celebrate or pass time. If a wolf leaves its pack will howl for him, and if he was a leader or close friend they'll howl longer. He won't howl for them though. Howling is a group activity.

Woodpecker tongues wrap around the back of their brains. Woodpecker tongues have a skeleton, and when retracted they wrap around the entire inside of their heads.

Worms have five hearts. Earthworms don't have mouths, eyes, arms, or faces, and they don't have a lot going on in their lives, but they do have five hearts. The distribution of body parts is one reason worms can sometimes regrow when cut in pieces.

Zebras can't sleep alone. Zebras have many predators who would love to eat them while they sleep. To keep this from happening they never sleep unless someone is nearby to guard them.

ACKNOWLEDGMENTS

I would like to gratefully thank Colin Dickerman, James Melia, Marlena Bittner, Steven Seighman, David Lott, and the whole team at Flatiron Books. Thanks to Duvall Osteen, the world's best agent. Thanks so much to Susan, Kim, Paige, Kieran, Drew, Bryn, and the rest of my family, for teaching me about animals and listening to me freak out about snow monkeys. Thanks to Boaz for everything. Thanks to Wieden+Kennedy and the people inside it, especially Jason, Smith, Megs, Susan, Amy, and Connery. And many thanks to everyone on the Internet, for making the Internet great and for emailing me depressing information about every animal imaginable. I'd also like to thank one of the birds at the Portland Audubon Society; he knows which one he is.